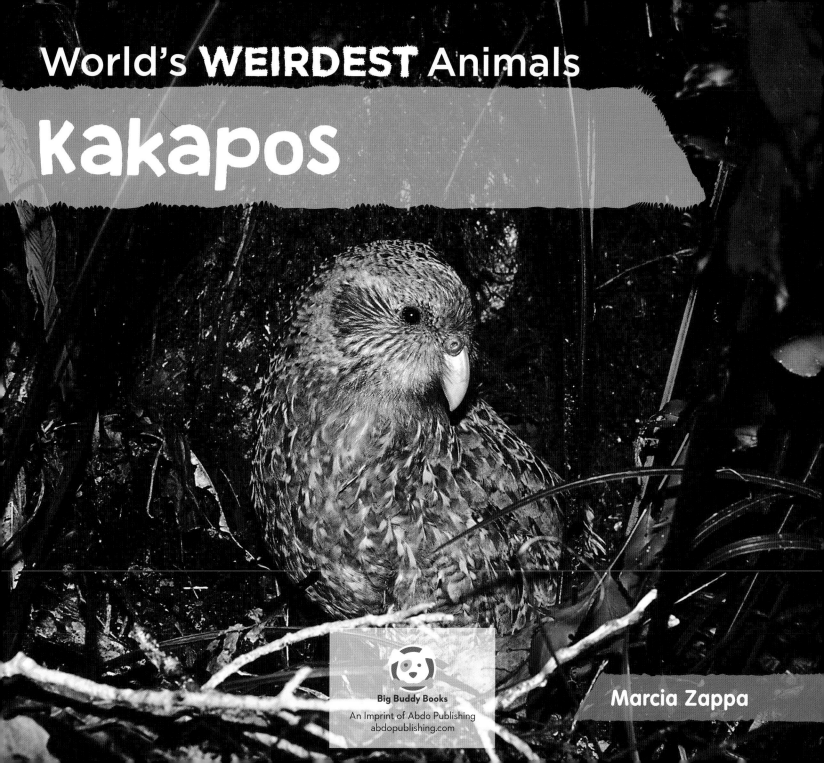

World's WEIRDEST Animals

Kakapos

Big Buddy Books

An Imprint of Abdo Publishing
abdopublishing.com

Marcia Zappa

abdopublishing.com

Published by Abdo Publishing, a division of ABDO, PO Box 398166, Minneapolis, Minnesota 55439. Copyright © 2016 by Abdo Consulting Group, Inc. International copyrights reserved in all countries. No part of this book may be reproduced in any form without written permission from the publisher. Big Buddy Books™ is a trademark and logo of Abdo Publishing.

Printed in the United States of America, North Mankato, Minnesota.
042015
092015

THIS BOOK CONTAINS
RECYCLED MATERIALS

Cover Photos: Robin Bush/Getty Images; Shutterstock.com.
Interior Photos: Glow Images (p. 11); Minden Pictures/AP Images (pp. 5, 7, 9, 17, 19, 21, 25, 27, 30); Shutterstock.com (p. 13); ©Geoff Moon/FLPA/Minden Pictures (p. 23); ©Brent Stephenson/NPL/Minden Pictures (p. 29).

Coordinating Series Editor: Rochelle Baltzer
Contributing Editors: Megan M. Gunderson, Sarah Tieck
Graphic Design: Adam Craven

Library of Congress Cataloging-in-Publication Data

Zappa, Marcia, 1985- author.
  Kakapos / Marcia Zappa.
      pages cm. -- (World's weirdest animals)
  ISBN 978-1-62403-776-4
1. Kakapo--Juvenile literature. 2. Parrots--New Zealand--Juvenile literature. I. Title.
  QL696.P7Z37 2016
  598.7'1--dc23

Contents

Wildly Weird!

The world is full of weird, wonderful animals. Kakapos (kah-kuh-POHS) are the world's heaviest parrots. They can't fly. They are **nocturnal**. And, they may live more than 50 years. These unusual features make kakapos wildly weird!

Kakapos are known for their strange looks and features.

Bold Bodies

The kakapo is a type of parrot. It has an unusual look. A kakapo's face is covered with a ring of pale feathers like an owl's. It has a short ivory beak.

Feathers cover a kakapo's body. Most are green. They have yellow, black, or brown bars or spots. A kakapo has a long, rounded tail. It has brownish-gray legs and feet.

Did You Know?

Most of a kakapo's feathers are very soft. They aren't used for flying. So, they don't have to be stiff like the feathers of other birds.

Big Birds

Large male kakapos can weigh more than eight pounds (3.6 kg). That is more than any other parrot! Kakapos store large amounts of fat for **energy**. This is unusual for land birds. Kakapos grow to be about two feet (0.6 m) long.

Some scientists believe that thousands of years ago, kakapos were light and flew like other parrots. But since they didn't have ground predators, they gained weight and started walking instead.

Strong Smell

Kakapos are known for giving off a strong smell. Some people say the odor is damp, but sweet.

Having a strong odor is important for **nocturnal** animals. It helps kakapos find each other in the dark. But, it can also help **predators** find them.

Kakapos have a powerful sense of smell.

Where in the World?

Long ago, kakapos were common in New Zealand. Humans first moved there in the 1200s. They destroyed the bird's **habitat**. They hunted kakapos. And, they brought new **predators**, such as stoats, rats, and cats.

Unlike the kakapo's original predators, these animals hunted on the ground. And, they often hunted by smell. Kakapos had no way to stay safe from them. Before long, many kakapos had died.

Did You Know?

Long ago, the kakapo's only predators were large birds of prey.

Stoats are a type of weasel.
They are skilled predators.

In the 1980s and 1990s, scientists took action to save this special bird. They moved them to islands off the coast of New Zealand. These islands have forests. And, they don't have the **predators** found on New Zealand's mainland. So, kakapos are much safer there.

Strange Birds

Kakapos live alone. They may screech or grunt to warn others to stay out of their home areas. And, they make "skraark" calls similar to other parrots.

Since they are **nocturnal**, kakapos sleep in trees or in hidden places on the ground during the day. At night, they search for food.

Kakapos are the only nocturnal parrots in the world.

Kakapos cannot fly. But, they still travel far. Kakapos have a jog-like walk. And, they climb trees! From the branches of a tree, they use their small wings to **glide** to the ground.

When a kakapo is scared, it freezes. Its feathers help it blend into its forest **habitat**. Long ago, this kept it safe from **predators**.

A kakapo usually stands with its body horizontal and its face near the ground. When scared, it stands up straight.

Favorite Foods

Kakapos eat plants that grow in their forest **habitat**. They eat fruits, seeds, leaves, stems, and roots. Today, kakapos also eat special pellets provided by scientists. These help keep the birds healthy for **breeding**.

Kakapos eat different plants during the year, depending on what is available.

Mating Calls

Male kakapos work hard to get the attention of females. They go to a special **breeding** area called a lek. There, they dig several small, shallow bowls into the ground.

Did You Know?

Kakapos only breed every two to four years, when there is plenty of food available.

Worn tracks lead to the bowls. This helps females find the males waiting there.

Males **compete** to have the best bowls. Once in a bowl, a male kakapo fills his body with air. Then, he makes a loud, low, booming call. This call can travel several miles.

After 20 to 30 booms, a male makes a high chinging call. These two calls can be heard for hours every night during **mating** season. A male stops calling after he has attracted a mate. This can take several months.

Did You Know?

The kakapo mating season is during summer and fall.

Often, males dig bowls on top of a hill or next to a large rock. Some scientists think this helps carry a mating call farther.

Life Cycle

A mother kakapo chooses a safe place to lay one to four eggs. This may be above ground in a nest hidden by plants. Or, it may be below ground in a natural crack or hole. After about a month, the eggs **hatch**. Kakapo chicks have white feathers.

After ten or more weeks, chicks are ready to venture out. But, mothers may continue feeding them for several more months.

Did You Know?

Kakapo eggs are white. They are about the size of chicken eggs.

Scientists closely watch kakapo chicks. They want to make sure all chicks grow up to be healthy adults.

World Wide Weird

Even though people continue working to save kakapos, they are still highly **endangered**. There are only about 125 kakapos living today.

It is important to know how our actions affect wild animals. Through change, we may be able to keep weird, wonderful animals such as kakapos around for years to come.

Scientists aren't sure exactly how long kakapos live. Many believe it is more than 50 years. Some think it may be more than 90!

FAST FACTS ABOUT:
Kakapos

Animal Type – bird

Size – about two feet (0.6 m) long

Weight – large males may weigh up to eight pounds (3.6 kg)

Habitat – forests on islands off the coast of New Zealand

Diet – fruits, seeds, leaves, stems, and roots

What makes the kakapo wildly weird?

It is the world's heaviest parrot, it can't fly, it is **nocturnal**, and it may live more than 50 years!

Glossary

breed to produce animals by mating.

compete to take part in a contest between two or more animals, persons, or groups.

endangered in danger of dying out.

energy (EH-nuhr-jee) the power or ability to do things.

glide to fall gradually without enough power for level flight.

habitat a place where a living thing is naturally found.

hatch to be born from an egg.

mate to join as a couple in order to reproduce, or have babies. A mate is a partner to join with in order to reproduce.

nocturnal active at night.

predator a person or animal that hunts and kills animals for food.

Websites

To learn more about World's Weirdest Animals, visit **booklinks.abdopublishing.com**. These links are routinely monitored and updated to provide the most current information available.

Index